T0159045

Little A And Uncle Thomas

John Chipley

Art by Tom Chipley

authorHOUSE®

AuthorHouse™
1663 Liberty Drive
Bloomington, IN 47403
www.authorhouse.com
Phone: 1 (800) 839-8640

Published by AuthorHouse 11/08/2018

ISBN: 978-1-5462-6810-9 (SC)
ISBN: 978-1-5462-6809-3 (HC)
ISBN: 978-1-5462-6811-6 (e)

Library of Congress Control Number: 2018913468

Print information available on the last page.

This book is printed on acid-free paper.

Contents

Dedicated to

"Sister"

1943 – 2018

The bus driver

Introduction

(On the first day of school, this was on my desk when I walked into the classroom)

Welcome to the eighth grade. I hope everyone had a fun and relaxing summer vacation. This morning, while I am working on getting our records set up in the school computer, I want you to write a two-page essay, double spaced, on what you did this summer. After lunch everyone will get a chance to introduce themselves and read their essay to the class. This will be both fun and your very first grade for the year, so give it your best. I will be grading your papers for spelling, grammar punctuation, and content. Take your time, have fun. You have all morning. WE ARE GOING TO HAVE A GREAT YEAR! Mr. Chip

Chapter #1

I just returned home from spending my summer with Uncle Thomas, known to everyone as, UT. My name is Abraham, known to everyone as Little-A. Let me tell you up front, I did NOT run away from home! I just didn't want to go to any more summer camps with only bug juice and graham crackers to eat and drink all day. Also, I didn't want to take orders from a teenager who was only one year older than me, and thought she was my master and I was her slave. No! I just didn't want to go there. So, I made other plans. I didn't run away, I just made other plans.

Just like every summer, when school was over for the year, Mom had ten-thousand summer camps lined up for me to attend. She handed me a piece of paper with my list of summer camps clearly outlined. **IT WAS HORRIBLE!**

- The Baptist Salvation for Youth Camp.
- The Methodist Work for Jesus Camp.
- The YMCA swimming camp.
- The Salvation Army feed the needy camp.
- The Boys and Girls Club summer play camp.
- The Service-to-Save Work Camp...

John Chipley

(And the list went on and on and on). That was when I decided to call for help. That was when I called UT.

Now, I didn't even know exactly where UT lived. I knew he lived some place in the state of Virginia, but I had no idea where Virginia was. I knew UT lived alone in a very small one room cabin on the top of a mountain, a very tall mountain. I had heard a lot of funny stories about my crazy white uncle. So, I figured, at the age of twelve, UT sounded like a better option for my summer adventures than more of the same-old-same-old children's summer camps. I wasn't a child anymore, I was twelve!

It was easy. I sent an e-mail to UT. And this is where my story begins. You might not believe what you're about to read. And I warn you, it is not for the wimpy reader. Plus, everyone knows I have a vivid imagination. But I promise you that every story is true: The bear story; the mountain people story (people who tried to kill me); the story about the gun, the very big gun; the story of driving UT's old car and hitting a tree; and the story of surviving with a crazy old man who took baths in his living room; and much much more. Some things I probably shouldn't have written about, but I did. After all, I was twelve and old enough to know what to do and what not to do.

It all started when I overheard my mom talking with one of her friends about my crazy uncle, Uncle Thomas.

Everyone called him UT. I had never met UT, but Mom had lots of crazy stories about him, and he sounded like a lot of fun to hang with over the summer. I knew where Mom kept UT's e-mail address. In fact, I knew where Mom kept everything. She just didn't know that I knew. I typed UT's address in on her computer and asked him if I could spend the summer with him. Almost immediately I received a reply; SURE. I will pick you up on Wednesday. Our adventure will start immediately.

WOW, I really wasn't expecting him to say, "SURE!" But he did! Now I had to somehow tell my mom what I did. And the timing of this conversation had to be perfect for me to get the right answer. Before Mom got home from work that evening, I had written my request to spend the summer with UT on a piece of paper and placed it inside an envelope. I addressed the envelope as, *"My dear Mom, we need to talk. Please open and read this AFTER supper."*

I knew that would get her attention. It also gave me time to write down exactly why it would be a good idea for her to let me spend the summer with UT, a man she did not trust or like. She never told me why she disliked him, and she refused to talk about it. It had something to do with why my dad went to prison and he didn't. I knew this wasn't going to be easy. Everything I wrote in my note to Mom had to be something positive. So, I wrote the note and then rewrote it, and rewrote it again, and kept rewriting it until it was letter perfect. I had to have a list of positive reasons for me to spend the summer with Uncle Thomas, positive reasons that Mom could not argue with. I did not lie, but I had to be creative with my words. I had to write the perfect letter.

I placed my letter inside the envelope, and that evening when I went to supper I placed the envelope on the table where everyone could see it. Mom looked at it and froze. She looked again and then looked over at me. She had this look on her face, as if I were in BIG trouble or something. It was all I could do to keep a straight face, but I did. I felt like a trial lawyer going to court to win my case. And, in a way, that was exactly what I was doing. I was trying to make a case for me to spend the summer with UT, a man described only as crazy. A man my Mom did not like.

My case had to be air tight. There was no room for error. Once Mom and Jasmine were seated, I said the blessing and started eating my dinner. I didn't say a word about the envelope, not one word. I just sat there and quietly ate my supper. I didn't look up. I just stared at my plate and slowly ate my supper. I could feel the tension in the room.

It was an extremely quiet dinner. Even my older sister, Jasmine, was quiet, and she was never quiet. If she wasn't talking, she wasn't breathing. Mom kept looking at me, then at the envelope, and then back at me. Jasmine ate her supper in about three bites, then she pushed back from the table, folded her arms, and sat there waiting to hear about what was in the envelop. She didn't jump up from the table and run to her room as usual. No. Tonight she just sat there and looked over the top of her glasses at me. Her expression seemed both angry and concerned. She sat and waited to hear about what was in the envelope. She probably thought I was going to rat on her about things she did while Mom was at work. This was becoming more fun than I had imagined, but I knew the game would not be over until Mom gave me permission to spend the summer with UT.

Once Mom finished eating, she stood up and started clearing the table. No one said a word. The envelope just sat there looking at us. Everyone was thinking, what was in the envelope? Mom stacked the dishes in the sink, carefully dried her hands on the dish towel, and walked back over to the table. She pulled out her chair and sat down. She slowly reached over and picked up the envelope. She held it in her hand and looked over at me. Then she slowly opened it. She started reading it to herself, then stopped. She looked over at me once again, and then began to read my letter out loud.

Chapter #2

Dear Mom,

You work very hard for us, and we never say thank you. So, this summer I want to thank you and save you a lot of money. Plus, I want to spend my summer reading and learning, not just swimming and eating junk food. I want to learn about life outside of Memphis and meet different types of people. I have asked Uncle Thomas if I could spend the summer with him, and he agreed. This will be a learning experience for me. It will help me learn more about our family and other parts of the United States. Education is a lot more than a classroom. I hope you will trust me enough to allow me to spend my summer with Uncle Thomas.

Love, Abraham

Mom just sat there, motionless, for about two minutes. Then she carefully stood up from her chair, looked over at me, grinned, started to laugh, then stopped. Then she slowly walked over to where I was sitting. She paused, then leaned over and gently whispered into my ear, **"ABRAHAM, NO WAY IN HELL!"**

Then she started laughing out loud and continued clearing off the table. And, that was that! Mom looked over at me, still laughing, and said, "Abraham, you know that UT is just a crazy old white man, don't you? He must be a hundred years old by now! What would you do all summer long on the top of a mountain with a crazy old man? I did tell you he was crazy, didn't I?"

Then she continued, "And how do you even plan on getting all the way from Memphis to Virginia? We don't have that kind of money. And, do you even know where Virginia is? Abraham, I trust you and love you, but sometimes parents are forced to make decisions that their children don't understand, and this, I am afraid, is one of those times. I'm sorry son, but I just can't let you do this. I'm sorry. You are too young, and UT is too old and way too crazy!"

I immediately stood up and shouted, **"BUT MOM, IT'S NOT FAIR!"**

Mom held up her hand, like a policeman stopping traffic, and replied, "Sorry Abraham, there are no buts. My decision is final. FINAL, do you understand!"

"BUT MOM, Uncle Thomas will be here Wednesday to pick me up."

Mom suddenly stopped doing the dishes. Her expression changed. Now she looked angry. She tossed the drying rag onto the floor and plopped herself back down at the table. She took out her cell phone and dialed UT's number. In a few minutes UT answered. Mom was telling Uncle Thomas, in a very firm voice, why I was too young to make such a long trip. Plus, the responsibility of looking after a boy my age was too hard for someone UT's age, and....... then suddenly she stopped. Then Mom got quiet. She looked at her phone and said, **"You are where?"**

Then there was a long pause. Mom looked over at me, as if I were in big trouble, and said, "Abraham, go open the front door."

I went to the front door and slowly opened it. There, bigger than life itself, stood this wild and crazy looking old white man. It was Uncle Thomas. I just stood there staring at him. Suddenly I wasn't sure I wanted to spend the summer with this strange looking old man. He was huge. His hair was white and long and wild. It ran half way down his back, like an Indian Chief. He wore a bright red scarf around his neck, and he had a gun. He had a BIG gun. It was in a holster that hung from around his waist and was tied to his leg as if he were some kind of western cowboy.

Then I heard Mom call out, **"Don't just stand there UT, come on in."**

UT laughed out loud and looked down at me. "Boy, you're not as big as I pictured you. But don't worry, by the end of the summer you'll be a lot bigger or, maybe, a lot smaller." Then he walked past me and sat down at the table with Mom. I glanced out the front door and couldn't believe what I saw. There, in front of our apartment, sat a motorcycle! **A REAL MOTORCYCLE.** A motorcycle with a side car.

I was so excited I couldn't wait. I ran outside and climbed onto the bike. I pretended that I was driving the bike. I pretended until I heard, **"ABRAHAM, GET OFF THAT BIKE, AND COME INSIDE."**

I went inside and sat at the table with Mom and Uncle Thomas. Uncle Thomas told Mom that he knew she would say, "NO!" So, he immediately got on the road, accompanied by his dog, BB, in the side car. I was so excited to see Uncle Thomas, I hadn't even noticed BB in the side car. BB was a great old dog. He had short black hair, long floppy ears, blue eyes, and seemed to understand what was happening. BB decided to stay in the side car. I think he knew what was about to happen and wanted to avoid the upcoming conflict between UT and my mom. Yes, BB was a very smart dog! And it didn't take long for the conflict to start. BB crawled down low in the seat and put both paws over his ears.

I went back inside the house and tried to help UT. I had to convince Mom that it was safe for me to spend the summer with Uncle Thomas. However, Mom's mind was made up. Plus, UT kept saying things that didn't help my cause. For example, he mentioned teaching me how to shoot a rifle. Mom hated any type of gun. So, that just killed everything. Mom didn't trust Uncle Thomas. She knew he was not bad, just different and crazy. She put on her parental face, used her VERY strong voice, and did what she thought was the adult thing to do. But I could see something in her expression, and heard something in her voice, that told me I just might have a chance, not a big one, but still a chance.

It took a long time to discuss the pros and cons of my living with Uncle Thomas. UT looked like a crazy man with his wild uncombed long white hair, but he really was a very kind old man. While he sat at the table talking to Mom, I saw a side of him I had never been told about. I actually began to feel sorry for him. He lived by himself on the top of a mountain, all alone. I don't think he was simply asking permission for me to spend the summer with him. No, I think he was asking permission for a young friend to spend some time with him, like a sleep over, only all summer. I think he was lonely. Yes, he was a bit crazy, but I saw an old man who needed me, and that was when I decided to make it happen! Sometimes a man has to do what a man has to do.

However, Mom still had not changed her mind. Her decision was final! But she did ask Uncle Thomas to stay for the night. However, he declined. He told Mom that there was too much work to do back home, and he couldn't live with so many people around him. He stood up, looked over at me and said, "Sorry boy, I tried. Maybe next year." Then he gave Mom and Jasmine a big hug and headed toward the front door. Everyone was sad, but being a parent isn't always easy. I didn't like Mom's decision, but I understood. One day I'll be a parent. One day I'll have a child to raise. One day I'll have to make adult decisions, BUT NOT TODAY. NO! TODAY I WAS ONLY TWELVE! TODAY I WAS GOING TO HAVE FUN BEING TWELVE!

So, while everyone was saying good-bye, I quietly went to my bedroom, shut the door, and crawled out my bedroom window.

Chapter #3

I quickly crawled into the sidecar. I pushed BB over to one side and curled up in a small space next to him. Then I placed UT's backpack on top of me. I thought I was hidden and no one could see me. BB and I were side-by-side and nose to nose in the bottom of the sidecar. BB knew what I was doing. He took one paw and placed it over my face, as to say, **"Be quiet, boy! you're just about free!"**

In a few minutes Mom and UT came outside. UT climbed onto his bike. He secured his helmet, then hit the start button. The sound of the motor made me jump with excitement. Then Mom suddenly noticed I wasn't there. She asked Uncle Thomas to wait, but UT looked down at BB, his backpack, and a pair of small feet, and replied, "No. Leave him be." He told Mom that I was probably somewhere crying, and it was probably best to leave me alone.

Then he waved good-by, turned his bike around, and gave it full throttle. With the sound of a jet airplane, we flew down the road that would, over time, take us to a small cabin on the top of a mountain somewhere in Virginia. As he pulled out onto the main road, UT said, "Little A, I know you're down there, I can see your feet. And you do know that you're about to get me in a heap of trouble." Then he laughed, and it was full speed ahead. My adventure had just begun. BB and I were both excited. This was too good to be true. This was going to be the best summer ever!

I left a note on my bedroom door that read, DO NOT DISTURB. Mom didn't know I was gone until hours later when I didn't show up for supper. Jasmine was sent to get me. She returned with a huge grin on her face and announced, "THANK YOU JESUS, HE'S GONE! Little A is gone, he has run away!"

Then she laughed out loud. She told Mom that I probably just ran away to my best friend's house down the street. Mom picked up the phone and called Enoch's house. To her surprise, I wasn't there. Then she found the note I left on my bed. It read, Dear Mom, I am with Uncle Thomas. I am fine. Please understand that I have to grow up. I love you. Have a great summer.

Mom just sat on the edge of my bed, speechless. Then she said, "That little rascal. How did he do it?" Jasmine continued laughing and thought the entire thing was very funny. Plus, she knew I would be grounded for the entire summer when I did come home. But I didn't come home. I was on the road with Uncle Thomas. This was the big escape, the big adventure, and very soon it became the big POLICE CAR!

We were about one hour out of Memphis, on I-40 heading east. I came out from under UT's backpack and sat up straight next to BB. My long cornrows were blowing in the wind, along with BB's ears. We must have made quite an impression on everyone that passed us, because everyone waved at us. Uncle Thomas told me to wave back. He told me it was what you did when you rode on (or in) a motorcycle, so I started waving. It was like being in a parade and more fun than any ride at the fair. People waved at us, honked their horns, and even yelled at us.

That was when I saw it, overhead. The electric sign over the interstate announced, **AMBER ALERT**. (This means a child has been kidnapped). I yelled at UT and pointed to the sign. UT couldn't hear what I was saying because of all the wind and motor noise, but he looked up. We both saw it at the same time. **BOY, ABRAHAM,**

AGE 12, AFRICAN-AMERICAN, WITH WHITE MAN ON 3-WHEEL MOTORCYCLE.

Just as soon as I saw the overhead sign, I heard a siren. I looked back and saw a patrol car with its blue lights flashing. It made a fast "U" turn across the interstate grass, and quickly sped in our direction. Uncle Thomas also noticed the police car and pulled over to the side of the road and stopped. At first, I thought this was the end of my summer adventure. I also thought, when I got home, I would be grounded for life! But I was pleasantly surprised. As it turned out, Uncle Thomas and I were not in trouble after all. It seemed as if all my work back home had paid off. Mom had had a change of heart. It was a real Thank-you Jesus moment.

Chapter #4

We both just sat there as the patrol car pulled up right behind us. The lights were flashing as if we had just robbed a bank. In a few minutes the officer slowly stepped out of his car, checked UT's tag number, and then walked over to the bike.

With a straight face UT asked, "Was I speeding?" The officer didn't smile. He replied, "Yes, however that is not why I stopped you." The officer asked, "Is this young man's name Abraham?"

UT looked surprised and said, "Well, yes it is. How did you know that?" The officer didn't find UT very funny. He just pointed at the overhead road sign, the **AMBER ALERT** sign. The sign that read, **12 YEAR-OLD AFRICAN-AMERICAN BOY, ABRAHAM, WITH WHITE MAN, ON 3-WHEELED MOTORCYCLE**. Uncle Thomas turned off his bike and said to the officer, "Can we talk?"

The officer, with a very serious expression on his face, said, "Sure, but I will do the talking, and you and Abraham will listen."

I knew when he said that, UT and I were both going to jail. UT didn't say a word, he just sat there. He sat there with his huge pistol strapped to his leg. The officer kept one eye on it but didn't say anything. That was when the officer pulled a piece of paper out of his pocket and, for the first time, smiled.

He said, "Abraham, this is a letter from your mom to you. She must be a very special lady. Listen to what she wrote."

Dear Abraham, I was wrong. I thought about what you wrote in your note to me, and you were right. You are growing up and you do need to experience life outside of our neighborhood. I am sorry you had to run away in order to achieve this experience, but I am not angry. However, over the summer I want you to read three books and write a book report on each book. I want each book report to be a minimum of two pages. I expect good grammar and spelling. Listen to your Uncle Thomas. He might be just a little crazy, but as you go through life you are going to meet a lot of crazy people. So, consider this adventure your Bar-mitzvah, (ask your uncle what a Bar-mitzvah is). See

you toward the end of August. Good luck
on your adventure. Love Ya, Mom.

Uncle Thomas just sat there, speechless. He glanced
over at BB and me. We were all speechless. That was
when the police officer started laughing. He told us that
Mom's letter was all over the internet. He told us that
he was instructed by his boss to escort us to the end of
Tennessee, with his lights on. He looked at me and told
me to be sure and wave at people. He said, "Abraham,
you and your crazy uncle are about to be in the longest
parade in the history of the United States." And with
those words, we continued our long journey across the
state of Tennessee.

Chapter #5

My summer adventure had begun, but I had no idea how much of an adventure I was about to experience. For now it was fun, lots of fun. As we rode down the interstate highway, behind the patrol car with its blue lights flashing, people started waving at us. Whenever we stopped for something to eat, restaurant owners wouldn't take our money. And at one point along our journey, a TV helicopter flew overhead and started recording our story. IT WAS TOTALLY AWESOME.

Mom's letter had made us famous! Plus, she had made herself famous. All she wanted to do was find me and let me know everything was okay. She wanted me to know that it was okay for me to spend the summer with Uncle Thomas. She knew that UT did not have a phone or TV. All he had was an old computer that didn't work most the time, so she called the police to help locate me and give me her letter. It all started out so simply, and then grew and grew and grew until UT, BB, and I were featured on the six o'clock news. All this over one letter from my mom, a letter that expressed the feelings of so many parents. A letter that said, **I was wrong. A letter that said, I can't stop you from growing up. A letter that said,** be careful, it's okay to jump and fly from the nest. But, most of all, it said if you do fall, I am always here to catch you. I love you.

As we came to the end of the state of Tennessee, the police officer pulled over and waved good-by as we passed into the state of Virginia. As I looked back I could see him standing next to his car waving. I waved back as we moved down the road and out of sight. Then UT pulled over to the side of the interstate. He said, "Little A, I have had all the attention I can stand. I think it's time for us to get lost in the mountains of Virginia. Then UT told me to hang on, and off we went up this narrow dirt road that seemed to be going straight up into the clouds, constantly turning left and right. Then we were at the top of a mountain.

Uncle Thomas stopped, looked left and right, then turned the motorbike off. Everything suddenly went quiet. UT pointed to the left and the many mountains that were still ahead of us. "Little A, can you see that mountain way over there? It's the tall one with the fire tower on the top of it."

I told him I could see it, but it looked like it was a long way away. UT replied, "Well, it is a long way, but that's where we're going. My cabin is right next to the ranger tower. If we hurry, we should be there by midnight." Then he hit the start button, the motor SCREAMED, and off we went. I soon learned that UT knew every small back road in the state of Virginia, and he didn't need a map. As we started down the side of the mountain, I was hanging on for dear life. He was driving like a MAD man! BB and I were almost flying through the air as we raced from dirt road to dirt road. My bottom was getting sore from bouncing over both rough roads and, sometimes, no roads. UT drove through open fields and shallow streams. Plus, he drove fast, way too fast!

All I could think about was how Mom told me that UT was crazy. Now I was beginning to understood what she meant. BB and I were hanging on to each other, and both of us were screaming at the same time. UT drove over mountain roads, and non-roads, as if he were........ crazy! Go figure!

When the sun went down, BB and I curled up in the bottom of the sidecar and tried to get some sleep. Sleep, however, was impossible. It was a long rough ride from where we were to where we were going. I wasn't having fun anymore. I hurt all over. Then, just as quickly as it started, it suddenly stopped. I stuck my head up from under BB's paws to see why we had stopped. UT pointed to a light in the distance. "See that light? That, Little A, is home."

What I saw in the distance was a very small cabin, a VERY small cabin. And, between us and the cabin was a VERY large river. It was too dark to see much beyond where we were parked. I was looking for a bridge, but there wasn't one. UT swung his leg over the bike and calmly stated, "Looks like they had a lot of rain while I was gone. I think we will have to leave the bike here and come back for it when the river goes down. We are going to have to walk the rest of the way."

I replied, "WALK? How far is it to your cabin? It looks a long way away."

Uncle Thomas looked down at me with a funny look, "How far," he replied. "Little A, it's not how far that's our problem. It's how DEEP."

I didn't understand. I asked, "What do you mean, how deep?"

"The river," he said. "I have no idea how deep the river is today."

Then he asked, "How tall are you?" I told him I didn't know. Then he asked me to get the rope out of the side car. I walked over, got the rope out and handed it to UT. He tied one end around my waist. Then he told me to start walking across the river. He told me to go slowly and watch my footing. Then he held onto the other end of the rope and slowly let it out as I walked into the ice cold and fast-moving river. As I walked, the river got deeper and deeper. This would have been dangerous on a good day, but it was night and it was very dark. I could hardly see my hand in front of my face. Then, suddenly, I slipped.

The water grabbed me like a tornado and pulled me under. I tried to stand up but couldn't. The force of the water pulled me back under and down- stream. I was breathing in more water then air. Every time I popped to the surface, all I could hear was UT yelling. The water was so loud I couldn't understand what he was yelling, but I was scared. My summer camp with UT hadn't even started, and I thought it was already over. All I could see was water and darkness. Then I felt a strong tug on the rope. I came to an immediate stop. The water had me trapped against a large rock. I couldn't move. I could see UT as he started moving into the water. He slowly made his way from one side of the river to the other. I couldn't move because my foot was stuck, and the water kept coming and coming, faster and faster, and deeper and deeper. Soon the water was up to my neck. I was now getting a little worried. No, I WAS A LOT WORRIED! Then I looked over and saw UT. To my surprise he was standing right next to me. He had tied his end of the rope to a tree and then followed the rope until he found me. He went under water and turned my foot sideways in order to free it from where it was stuck. He grabbed my arm and told me to climb up onto his back. Then he pulled us both to safety. He just laughed and said, "Well, Abraham, I guess we've had our baths for today. Are you okay?"

I told him I was fine, but the truth was I was cold, very cold. Plus, I was wet and tired and hungry and scared, and we still had a long walk ahead of us up the side of the mountain, before we reached UT's cabin. But I was determined to not let UT know how I really felt. After all, he was an old man, and I was a strong young boy. Surely, I could keep up with an old man.

UT's cabin was on the very top of the mountain, and the climb was almost straight up. I was now out of energy and my foot was beginning to bleed. Just then, when I thought things couldn't get any worse, they suddenly did. Through the darkness I heard a sound, a very loud sound! Something was coming through the woods in our direction. It was big, and it was moving at a high rate of speed.

I hung onto Uncle Thomas, like fleas on a dog. UT told me to not say a word. Everything, he repeated, was okay, but I knew things were **NOT** okay! I watched as UT slowly pulled his huge long barreled pistol out of its holster. He propped it with both hands and was ready for whatever was coming in after us. Then I heard a voice. It was the forest ranger, Smokie.

He was yelling at UT to not shoot. UT laughed and lowered his pistol. UT's BIG pistol was shaking. Uncle Thomas YELLED, "Smokie, you scared the P-Jesus out of me!" (Smokie was the ranger who took care of the fire tower next to UT's cabin). He saw us making our way toward the cabin and figured we might need some help. When he came running out of the darkness, I thought it was a bear. Smokie was HUGE. He made UT look skinny. Smokie started laughing, picked me up with one hand, like a rag doll, and tossed me onto his back. Then off we went straight up the side of the tallest mountain I had ever seen. Smokie was climbing straight up, hand over hand, and I was hanging on around his neck for dear life. When we reached the top, he lowered me to the ground. I was so tired I couldn't stand up. UT picked me up and took me inside. He laid me on his bed, covered me up with several blankets, and I was asleep before he could get a fire started in his old iron wood-burning stove, a stove he named Annie. Annie was the name of his wife who died many years ago. Now the new Annie continued to kept UT warm and provided him company.

Smokie stayed with us that night. He was afraid I was too cold, and my foot looked too swollen. As a ranger, he had lots of training in first-aid. He kept testing me for a fever all night. In the morning he wrapped my foot to stop the bleeding and help the swelling go down. Neither Smokie nor UT slept that night. They both just sat next to Annie and talked. I would wake up from time to time and could hear them telling tall tales to each other and laughing. I had never felt so protected or so safe as I did that night. And that was just the first night. The next morning proved to be just as interesting.

Chapter #6

That next morning, I woke up to the sound of UT and Smokie talking about a bear Smokie saw two days ago. When I opened my eyes, I also saw my clothes hanging over the back of a chair next to Annie. They were in the process of drying. That was when I realized all I had on was UT's very large undershirt. It fit me like a dress or nightshirt.

When I finally crawled out of bed Smokie asked how I felt. Then he checked me again for a fever. He told me that I got too cold last night from the river. I was shaking and starting to go into hyperthermia. *[Hyperthermia is when the body gets too cold and the organs inside the body start to die]*. So, he and UT removed my cold wet clothes, wrapped me in a blanket, and laid me on the floor next to Annie. I was so tired I never woke up, but I felt fine in the morning. I joined Smokie and UT for a strong cup of morning coffee.

UT didn't know that I had never had coffee before. UT didn't know a lot about the rules of raising kids, and I liked that. He talked to me and treated me as if we were both adults. I decided not to tell him I was only twelve. I also decided I wasn't going to tell him all the rules Mom had for me to follow! NO! I was going to have a summer full of NO RULES!

After breakfast, Smokie said good-by and left the cabin to start his climb up the fire tower that stood next to UT's cabin. One part of his job was to climb to the top of the tower once every day and look for potential forest fires. He had to climb up over 100 steps to reach the top. Just as he left to start his climb, UT tossed me the keys to his old car and asked if I would drive down to the country store at the bottom of the mountain and bring him back the morning paper.

Once again, I didn't tell UT that I had never driven a car before. I figured, how hard could it be? So, I pulled on my warm clothes and went outside to find UT's car. The good news was his car was very old and had lots of dents all over it. I figured I couldn't do too much more damage to it. When I got inside the car I was surprised to find BB asleep in the back seat. I didn't know how he got across the river, but he did. Now he was about to take a ride down the mountain road with me to get UT a paper.

I put the key in the ignition and turned it. The motor slowly turned over, as if it were not sure it wanted me to be driving. My legs were too short to reach the pedals, so I looked around for something that might help. I spotted a chair cushion over on the porch and placed it at my back. PERFECT! This was going to be fun. I knew where the gas and brake pedals were. The shifting lever looked easy to work, so I put it in D (for drive), took a deep breath, and took my foot off the brake. The car started moving down the gravel driveway and out onto the gravel country road. But I had a problem. I was moving too fast. I put my foot back on the brake pedal, but the car didn't slow down. Instead, it started going faster. I was turning the steering wheel left and right, trying to stay on the road. On both sides of the road were huge ditches. The car continued to pick up speed as we moved further and faster down the mountain road. I continued to put my foot on the brake pedal over and over and over. Nothing worked. The car continued to move faster and faster and faster. I knew that if I continued down the winding mountain road at a faster and faster pace I would eventually crash. I had to stay calm and figure out how to stop the car. That was when BB jumped into the front seat next to me. I yelled at him, "WELL, BB, WHAT DO I DO?"

Then, as if he understood me, he put his paw on the ignition key. PERFECT! I reached over and turned off the car. Suddenly we started going slower and slower. I could now keep it on the winding dirt road, but we were still moving too fast. Then, just as we rounded the last turn, I saw the country store in the distance. Now all I had to do was figure out how to stop the car, not just go slower. Then, just as if God were watching over me, I saw a boy driving a tractor. He pulled out onto the road right in front of me. He was pulling a trailer full of hay, and, suddenly, one of the hay-bails came loose and fell onto the road right in front of UT's car. PERFECT! I hit it dead-center! UT's old car came to a messy and sudden halt.

UT's car was covered with hay, but the car was stopped. The boy jumped off the tractor and came running back to the car to make sure I was okay. Hay straw was everywhere, both outside and inside the car. He removed the hay from the window, stuck his head inside, and asked, **"Who are you?"**

I told him, "Abraham, but everyone just calls me Little **A. Who are you?**"

He said, "My name is Henry-Joshua Miller, but everyone just calls me Joshua." Joshua, I discovered, liked to be funny. He was like the class clown, only he didn't go to school. His mom believed in teaching him and his sister at home. His school didn't have walls, instead it had over one-hundred acres of farm land. Joshua even had his own special library. He loved to read, and he read everything.

Joshua looked like a country boy, tall and skinny. He didn't wear a shirt. I could count every one of his ribs.

He was white, or maybe dirty white. He had a country-boy looking haircut, bare feet, and wore bib-overalls. In the mountains that was what all the boys wore. Joshua also talked funny, and he talked a lot. He looked at me and said, "Little A, ain't many colored folks up here in these mountains. I can think of only two."

I didn't know what to say, but I wasn't going to let him get the last word. I replied, "Well, there aren't many white folks where I live! **Is my color going to be a problem for you? If it is, you can paint me any color you want. Does the store have any paint?"**

Joshua ignored my question, and I won the first war of words. Then he asked, "Are you here with your mom and dad for summer vacation?"

"HELL NO." I replied, "I ran away from home! I'm going to join the circus and see the world. I'm here by myself, and the police are looking for me."

Joshua got excited, **"YOU RAN AWAY!** Your Papa go'na kill you when you get home."

I replied, "I don't have a dad."

Joshua tilted his head downward, as if he were looking over his glasses, and said in a very teacher type manor, "No dad? Little A, everyone got a dad. You got to have a mom and dad just to be born. You do know about the sperm and the egg thing, don't you? They did teach you that in y'ur fancy city school didn't they? Or do they not talk about such things? One day I'm going to be a doctor. I need to know 'bout all those things. I already know the names of every bone in the body, and I know most of the major organs."

Joshua was trying to out-smart me. He was messing with me, and I knew it. But I was good at this game. I sat up straight in the seat of UT's car, so that I looked taller and smarter than I really was. "I know all about sex. I know a lot more than you do! Plus, I'm the fastest runner in my school. I know the entire multiplication table, and all the states and capital cities of the United States. And about my dad, I don't have a dad because he died in prison. He killed a man with his bare hands. He ripped his head right off his body. And if you mess with me, I just might do the same thing. What does **YOUR** dad do?"

Now, even though my answer wasn't totally true, it was designed to make me look tough, and it did stop Joshua for a few minutes. Then things got quiet, too quiet. There was a long pause. Joshua said, in a voice that I could hardly hear, "Truth is I don't have no dad. My mom and dad died in a car accident. I live with Ms. Pervis and Betsy. Ms. Pervis owns the store, but only strangers call her Ms. Pervis. Everyone around here just calls her Sister. I don't know why everyone calls her Sister. I think it has something to do with the old man who lives on the top of the mountain. She never talks about it and I don't ask any questions. She is getting old and a little strange, but she's good to me and Betsy. She is the only mom I remember. She and Betsy are my family."

I quickly realized that I had said the wrong thing. I felt terrible. I had to do something that would make Joshua feel better. So I said, "Joshua, it's okay. Neither one of us has a dad, so that makes us alike. Now, let's get back to my skin color. Exactly what color do you want to paint me?"

Joshua started laughing and said, **"How about PINK, like a pig, like a pink city pig!"** He was making fun of me, but I didn't care. I felt bad about what I said. I shouldn't have said it. So, I went along with his game plan.

I said, **"Perfect. I'll be right back."** I turned and walked into the country store and asked the girl standing behind the counter if she had any paint. She told me she did. So, I asked for a can of pink paint.

"PINK?" she replied. "I don't think we have any pink paint, how about yellow or ...." Then she paused.

"Wait," she said, "I just might have a can of pink paint." She turned and went into the back room of the store and returned with a can of pink paint. She told me that a lady ordered this can of pink paint over a year ago and never picked it up. She said I could have it, free. Then I asked her for two paint brushes. She got this funny look on her face, as if she knew I was up to no good. Then she handed me two paint brushes. I thanked her, took the paint and brushes outside and handed them to Joshua. Then I stood there, in the middle of the dirt road, right in front of the country store, and took off my clothes. Right there in front of the country store I stood totally naked. I told Joshua, **"Okay, country boy, paint me pink."**

Joshua started laughing. He laughed so hard he couldn't open the can of paint, so I opened it for him. While I opened the can, he took off his clothes. We each grabbed a brush and started painting the other person pink from head to butt to toe. When we finished, we laughed so hard we cried. The girl in the store came running outside to see what all the noise was about. She just stood there and shouted, **"Joshua!** Sister's going to kill you! You two boys must be crazy."

As for Joshua and myself, our game of words had ended. After our exchange of insults and one gallon of pink paint, we had become best friends. I recommend this to anyone who is having a problem with another person. Standing nude with another person while painting each other pink, (or any color) gives you time to think. It also gives you even more time to laugh. And it's impossible to be angry at someone when you're laughing.

Chapter #7

When we finished painting each other, Sister came outside and handed each of us some soap and a towel and told us to go wash off the paint in the pond behind the store. She said we had to get the paint off before it dried.

Joshua and I went around to the back of Sister's store and jumped into the pond. Once we washed off the paint and returned to our natural colors, we walked over behind UT's car, where we had laid our clothes, and got dressed. When I walked out from behind UT's car, I noticed her, the girl who worked in Sister's store. She looked to be about my age, African-American, tall, skinny, long braids, and beautiful.

She was standing on the front porch of the store just watching me. "Hi, Pinky," she shouted, "I'm Betsy. The stupid little boy you just painted pink is my brother."

I was suddenly embarrassed. Sometimes growing up is just that quick. Suddenly I noticed a girl and she looked different from all other girls. I could feel it. I knew I was in love before I even knew what love was. I just knew it, and, I discovered later, Betsy also knew it.

Joshua started removing all the straw from the front of UT's car, while I went into the store to get UT a paper. When I asked Betsy for a newspaper, I realized I didn't have any money. She handed me a paper and said, "Never seen a nude pink boy before." She laughed, and then, with a straight face, said, "You know, all you boys look the same, regardless of color." Then she laughed at me, not with me, **at me!** She undressed me with her words. I didn't know what to say.

Her words embarrassed me, and, at the same time, made me laugh. I knew she was having fun messing with me, and, frankly, I enjoyed it. She could have said anything, and I wouldn't have cared. I had never felt what I was now feeling, and I liked it. I liked it a lot!

I stood there in the store, a very confused little boy. I couldn't say anything. I tried to talk, but words just wouldn't come out. Plus, I didn't know what to say. Even though I was wearing my clothes, I held my hands over the front of my pants, as if that would help. She noticed. She looked at me and, once again, started to giggle. I tried to act normal, but it wasn't possible.

Then, just like that, she asked, "Are you visiting someone or just passing through town painting people pink along the way?"

She was good with words, and again I tried to keep a straight face but couldn't. I started laughing and this time couldn't stop. Finally, I got control of myself and told her about how I was spending the summer with my uncle, Uncle Thomas. When I said that, she said, **"The old man on the mountain top? That old man is your uncle? You do know that he's crazy, don't you!"** Then she went over the cash register and told me the paper and two brushes would be $7.58. That was when I discovered I didn't have any money.

"That's okay," she said, "I'll just put it on your uncle's tab." Then she asked, "Are you the boy whose momma wrote the letter saying she was wrong about you spending the summer with your uncle? Is that You? Is that crazy man your uncle? The story was in the paper and on the news. Everybody knows about you."

She told me that following the article in the paper, lots of people stopped by their store and asked for directions to where Uncle Thomas and the city boy lived. She told me that everyone wanted to see me, UT, and his cabin. She said that she didn't tell anyone about where UT lived. She knew he was a very private person, and always carried a pistol as big as a rifle. She told me that she didn't want anyone to get hurt.

She said, "However, our sales doubled. So, Pink boy, tell your uncle that because he's so famous and you're so cute, he gets this paper free, along with the paint brushes."

Then she just stood there staring at me, and I just stood there staring at her. In a very quiet and submissive voice, I said, "My name is Abraham, not pink boy. But everyone just calls me Little A." She didn't say anything. She didn't say hello, or nice to meet you, or anything. The store became very quiet. I could hear the clock ticking on the wall, like a heartbeat. Then, like a stupid little boy, I said, "You're beautiful."

I couldn't believe I just said that! I didn't mean to say it out loud. I meant to say it to myself. But it was too late. The words were already out of my mouth.

Then, with a soft tone in her voice, she replied, "Little A, so are you."

I stood there frozen like a Roman statue, unable to move or talk. Then I turned and ran out of the store. I ran as if I were running away from something I couldn't run away from.

By this time, Joshua had removed all the straw from off the front of UT's car and was sitting on the hood waiting for me to return. He told me to come over to his house anytime. He said he was always working, but I could help.

Joshua pointed to an old farm house that sat way back off the road. He told me that was where he lived. It was Sister's house and farm. He told me that she adopted him after his parents died in a car accident. At the time he was only one year old. A year later she adopted Betsy. Joshua said that he and Betsy grew up together, like brother and sister. Sister and Betsy were the only colored people on the mountain. Sister was very much like Uncle Thomas. She was a free spirit, like a child, and loved every animal that showed up at her farm house. She had more cats than I could count, and she called each of them by name. However, her dog, Morley, was her favorite. He was a small framed scruffy mutt that looked very much like BB. Morley went everywhere Sister went. She fixed him food as if he were a king. Morley never ate dog food. He only ate human food, and he ate very good human food. Sister loved to cook.

Sister loved everyone, and everyone looked after Sister. Sister wasn't crazy, but she was, well, different. She never cleaned the house. As soon as Betsy and I were old enough, we started doing all the house work. Sister just never seemed to see that the dishes were dirty, or the papers and bills were stacked all over the floor here and there. And, if one of her many cats didn't show up for dinner, she would worry herself sick about it. When the cat would show up, two or three days later, she would always have a party to celebrate. Yes, Sister was a little different, but I loved the difference. I think everyone loved the difference.

The farm house Joshua pointed to looked old and tired. It seemed to be leaning in one direction, as if a good wind might blow it over. The house had never been painted a color. The wood siding had turned brown or grayish in color from age, but it had a bright red tin roof that looked almost new.

Joshua jumped off the hood of UT's car, climbed back up onto the tractor, and continued slowly driving down the road. We were now brothers. We had insulted each other, tried to out talk each other, and painted each other pink. This is the kind of crazy stuff brothers do.

Chapter #8

I turned UT's car around, hitting only one small tree in the process. Because it was a small tree it only made a small dent. And, as I said earlier, the car was already covered with dents, so my new dent just blended in with all the others.

The drive back up the dirt road was much slower. When I came to UT's driveway I made a sharp turn to the right and stopped. His driveway was almost straight up. I sat there for a few minutes and just looked at the challenge. Then I pushed the accelerator to the floor and I shot up the hill like a rocket. I came to a stop just before hitting the side of UT's cabin. But I could tell by the marks on the side of his cabin that Uncle Thomas had hit the side of his cabin many times.

When I gave UT the paper he told me that the brakes on his car didn't always work. He told me to pump the brake pedal two or three times, then they might work. I decided not to tell Uncle Thomas about almost hitting Joshua's tractor and running into the straw bale. However, I did tell UT about me not having any money and about meeting Joshua, Betsy, and Sister. Uncle Thomas had already started reading the paper. I told UT about Joshua and how we painted each other pink. All Uncle Thomas said was, "Why pink," and continued reading his morning paper. I don't think he heard anything I said. He was lost in his paper. I had a lot to learn about UT. I didn't think Uncle Thomas was crazy, but he was a little strange. And I loved the strangeness.

I could tell it was going to be an interesting summer. While I loved Uncle Thomas' craziness, I was beginning to wonder if summer camp in Memphis might have been a better choice. But I had made my choice, and I was going to stay with the game plan. Only, I didn't know what UT's game plan was. No one seemed to know what UT's game plan was. Even Uncle Thomas didn't know what his game plan was. All I knew, so far, was everyone kept telling me Uncle Thomas was crazy, and I needed to always keep an eye on his pistol. The BIG one. The one with the LONG BARREL. The one he always wore. And I always wondered exactly how crazy he really was. However, I did always keep an eye on his pistol.

UT sat quietly and read every word of the Washington Post paper. It was as if I weren't even there. He made it very clear that he was not going to be a camp counselor, parent, or baby sitter. And he didn't have many rules. However, we did have one meeting. When he finished the paper, he looked over at me and told me, "Abraham, I do not know why you wanted to spend the summer with me. You don't even know me. People tell me that I'm crazy, and I probably am. But you are my brother's son, and I am honored that you wanted to spend some time with me."

Then he got serious. "Abraham, we have to talk. There are rules of living alone on the top of a mountain. These are not my rules, I don't have any rules. These are the basic rules of survival, and we can start with the car."

I stood up and walked over and sat next to where UT was sitting. He said, "You had never driven a car before, had you?"

I told him, "No."

Then he said, "But you did it. And you made it all the way to the store and back home on your own. That's the way people learn. In the mountains, to survive, you have to learn things very fast. And you do things you never thought you could do. This is why I love it, and tonight will be a good example. Tonight, for supper, we are going to have squirrel stew. I'll bet you've never had squirrel stew, have you?"

I replied, "**CORRECT**! And I don't think I want to start."

UT just looked at me and said, "Okay, you don't have to eat anything you don't want to eat. When you get hungry your body will tell you to eat. However, squirrel stew is for supper tonight, and you are going to love it, but first we have to kill three squirrels. Abraham, you can't buy squirrels at the store, so we kill our own." UT stood up and walked over to the door that led to a small deck attached to the side of his cabin. Down below the deck, in the woods, there were lots of animals running around. UT told me to bring him his 22-rifle. It was propped against the wall next to his bed. Then he said, "Abraham, this is how one goes shopping when they live on the top of a mountain."

I walked over and handed UT the rifle. He told me to have a seat on the deck next to him and watch. He said I could shoot the second squirrel. I sat in the chair next to UT and watched as we propped the barrel of the rifle on the porch railing and waited. Soon I saw a squirrel running out of the woods. UT took aim and pulled the trigger. With one shot, the squirrel was dead. Then he handed me the rifle.

I tried to sound tough, so I shouted, "**Damn**, UT, you're good."

Uncle Thomas looked over at me. "Abraham," he said, "I know city boys use words like that, but I don't want you to curse up here. It hurts my ears. I read a quote years ago that said, '*bad words create storms*'. I tend to agree.

Words tell people who you are. And you, Abraham, are a lot better than Damn. Are you okay with this.?"

I felt terrible. I was embarrassed. All I could say was, "Sure. I'm sorry."

All UT said was, "It's okay, Abraham. This is how people learn. Things are just different up here. Before the summer is out, you will also be different. I think it will be impossible for you not to change."

Then he showed me how to prop the barrel of the rifle on the porch railing and wait for the right moment. UT told me that that was the most important thing for me to learn about hunting, patience. He told me to wait for the shot. He said, "Wait for the squirrel to freeze." He told me that squirrels seemed to know when something is wrong. Once the squirrel is still, and its tail stops moving, pull the trigger! He told me to aim for the body, and hope I hit something.

Just then I saw a squirrel. The squirrel ran across the back open area close to the deck and then stopped. It looked at me. I could see it looking at me. Then its tail froze. The squirrel knew. I knew. The squirrel was alive that morning and planning on living many more good days until I pulled the trigger. It flipped in the air from the force of the bullet. It made a sound that I can hear to this day. I had just killed another living thing, and I would soon be eating it.

I didn't feel proud or excited or manly or anything. I had just killed something. I had never done that before. And UT let me kill the third squirrel. It wasn't hard. In fact, it was very easy, too easy. Killing wasn't fun, it was necessary.

After the killing came the hard part. The hard part is called the dressing. This is where you cut the squirrel open along the bottom side. Then you remove the guts from the meat, and the meat from the furry skin. UT had to do this. I couldn't do it. Cutting open the squirrel was too gross. However, I learned by watching. I was learning basic survival skills. I was learning things they didn't teach in school, and I was learning more. I was learning about how all animals kill, even human animals. Sometimes we kill for survival, sometimes for sport, and sometimes we kill out of anger. Humans are the ONLY animals who kill out of anger.

I learned a lot that day, but most of all I learned that words can hurt people just like bullets. After that day, I never used the word damn, ----- Never! For some reason it hurt my ears.

UT put an iron skillet on top of Annie. He placed the squirrel meat in the skillet. Then he added oil, wine, potatoes, water, and onions. He put a lid on the top and let it cook all afternoon. And, while it was cooking, we made bread. I had never made bread before. I thought you had to buy bread from a store. However, making bread was both easy and fun. We used flour, water, and a few eggs. Then we mixed it all together using our hands. It was easy, and the best tasting bread I had ever eaten. That night, for supper, we had squirrel stew and fresh bread. WONDERFUL! And we did it without having to go to the store. Plus, Betsy showed up with an apple pie as a welcoming gift to me. And, most importantly, she stayed and had supper with us. It was all so much fun, so great. After supper it was beginning to get dark, so UT asked me to walk Betsy home. Betsy and I walked and talked and laughed all the way to her farm house. Sister was waiting for Betsy on the front porch. When she saw me walking with her, coming toward the house, she got up and went inside. Betsy and I stood on the front porch for a long time not saying anything. I felt like the squirrel that froze before being shot. Then I told Betsy I had better get home. When I said that, she said, "**WELL, aren't you going to kiss me?**"

At first, I couldn't answer. I just stood there, like a squirrel, frozen. Then I finally said, "I've never kissed a girl before? Is it O.K?"

Then Betsy admitted, "Well, I've never kissed a boy." Then she leaned over and kissed me. She smiled and said, **"Yes, it's O.K."** Then she turned and walked inside. **WOW!** Uncle Thomas told me he heard me singing as I was walked up the road toward his cabin.

That night I went to sleep while UT read to me from one of his many books. He didn't have a TV, just a wall full of books. He had books on every subject from art to guns to Tom Sawyer. That night I selected a book about Tom Sawyer. I crawled in bed and UT sat next to the wood burning stove, Annie, and started reading. Then he stopped. He said, "Abraham, you like Betsy don't you?"

All I said was, "UT, you're sounding like my mom."

Uncle Thomas just smiled and continued reading. I was asleep before he finished the first page. This was the beginning of my great summer adventure. This was the summer of my coming of age.

Chapter #9

Very early the next morning I woke up to the sound of UT dragging a metal tub inside the house. It was a very large metal tub, about the size and shape of a small bath tub! I watched from my bed as he placed it next to Annie and started filling it with water. His cabin did not have any hot water, so he would put a small bucket of water on top of Annie and heat it up. Then he would dump it into the big tub. He did this over and over and over. Once the tub was about half full he told me that I could take my bath first, while the water was still warm and clean.

I looked over at him and asked, "Don't you have a bathroom, or a shower?" He laughed and said, "Nope. I only have one room. That's all I need. You're going to have to get used to seeing a naked old fat man from time to time. "Sorry," he said. "Guess I should have told you. I just didn't think about it. I'm old, Abraham, I don't think about things like I used to. When you asked to spend the summer with me all I thought about was the fun we would have. I didn't think about how different it would be for you."

Nothing seemed to bother Uncle Thomas, nothing. He was always just having fun. And he always talked to himself out loud, like he was telling himself what to do. I think he did this because he lived alone and just needed someone to talk to. Yes, UT really was a crazy funny old man.

"Well," he said, "are you going first, or am I?"

UT only had to ask once, I jumped out of bed, took off my pajamas, and climbed into the tub. UT handed me some soap, and I had my first cabin bath. And, just like last night's supper, it was great. I sat in the tub, next to the heat of Annie, and washed and watched as UT fixed us something to eat. We had eggs from his own chickens and left-over homemade bread from last night. Best breakfast I ever ate!

Everything at UT's cabin was different from what I was used to seeing back home. Everything was so simple. We both worked all day, but it didn't feel like work. It felt like fun. UT didn't even have a clock. He didn't live by the clock, he lived by the day. We would get up when the sun came up, or whenever we wanted to get up. We went to bed when we got tired. There was no such thing as saying, "It's your bed time." There was no bed time. And, there was no TV. We read to each other every night. Some nights we just talked. Some nights I fell asleep right after supper. Some nights UT fell asleep before supper. Everything just happened in its own time. It was so quiet, so peaceful. It was like living in slow motion. It was like walking and never running. There was no rush to do anything.

One morning I woke up and just lay in bed thinking about where I was and what I was doing. I was a long way from home. I was a long way from all my friends. Everything was so different. I loved Uncle Thomas' cabin. It really was high up on the top of a mountain. The road to his cabin was almost straight up. And his cabin was just one room. YES, just one room! His workshop, and motorcycle, took up one half of the room. YES, he kept his motorcycle inside the cabin. Annie, the iron wood-burning stove, was both the heater and a cooking stove for the cabin. There was a deck on one side. This was where we sat and talked and watched the animals as they walked through the woods. UT seemed to know the animals almost by name.

UT's car was as old as he was, and, same as UT, very dented from age and misuse. I think UT must have hit almost every tree in the woods. Of course, UT also had his three-wheel motorbike. He used the motorbike on pretty days and the old car on rainy days. The bike was what I rode in all the way from Memphis to his cabin in Virginia. And there was BB, his dog. BB was a black short haired mutt, and a very smart mutt. BB loved to sleep with me, and I loved sleeping with BB. However, BB was a country dog and could smell a dear a mile away and start barking at any time, day or night. That was a problem at night. However, UT would just open the door and let her run. She always returned in the morning. She never told me about her adventures, and I was glad to get some sleep. But one morning she didn't return, and I could tell that UT was worried. Later that morning UT took his rifle and started walking into the woods. It wasn't long before I heard a shot, then another. Then I saw BB running toward the cabin, and UT was slowly walking behind her. I never knew what happened. I had learned not to ask too many questions. There were things, according to Uncle Thomas, that I just didn't need to know. But BB told me everything that night before going to sleep. If you know how to listen, dogs can talk.

The next morning started with thunder and rain, lots and lots of rain. It was so loud I could hardly hear UT talking. Water was running down the mountain and past the cabin like a river. UT and I stood out on the deck, in the summer rain, and took advantage of the rain by taking an outdoor shower. I know, it sounds crazy, but it was fun. I had never taken a shower outside before. While taking my outdoor shower, I glanced over and watched as the water washed UT's old car down his driveway and then down the gravel road. UT wasn't surprised or angry, he thought it was funny. He told me this happened all the time. He would wait for the rain to stop, then go looking for his car. Many times, he told me, he got Joshua to help him pull his car out of a ditch and back onto the gravel road. UT acted as if that were normal, as if everyone went looking for their car after a heavy rain and everyone took showers outside. It didn't take long for me to relax and just be me. I was beginning to change. I could feel myself just having fun. I was beginning to enjoy my mountain summer camp experience with Uncle Thomas.

Chapter #10

Weeks went by and I started blending into the mountain life as if I were born there. One morning I told UT I was going to walk down to Joshua's house and see what he was doing. Uncle Thomas started laughing. "Abraham," he said, "are you going to see Joshua or Betsy?"

I had to laugh. UT could read me like a book. I told him, "Betsy, of course." UT just rolled his eyes, and said he had to go to town and pick up a few things, and we would catch up with each other around supper time. We each went our own way. Uncle Thomas knew where he was going, but I wasn't sure as to where I was going. However, I had a long walk to Betsy's house and time to think about both Joshua and Betsy. I had time to think about a lot of things. I even thought about not going home. I knew this was crazy, but I still thought about it.

The mountains were different from what I was used to back home. Mom would never let me just go somewhere and say, "We will catch up around supper time." Like I said before, I don't think Uncle Thomas knew anything about raising kids, and I liked it that way.

It took about an hour to walk down to the bottom of the mountain, but it was a beautiful day with lots of things to look at and explore along the way. There wasn't any rush. Like I said earlier, mountain life is like living in slow motion.

When I reached Joshua's house I saw him on the tractor plowing the back field, a long way from where I stood. So, I stepped inside the country store to say hello to Betsy. She was putting up stock. She stopped and walked over to the counter where I was standing. "**Well, hello Pinky.**" She giggled and looked at me all over. Her eyes were easy to read, as well as my embarrassment. I could tell that she now had a new name for me. She was the only girl who had ever seen me pink; no clothes, just pink. And I knew she was not going to let me forget it.

I told her I had come over to help Joshua with his chores. This was a lie, of course, but it gave me something to say. I told her I'd see her later and then turned and walked out the store as if she wasn't special. I walked down the dirt road that led over to Sister's house and sat on the front porch. It didn't take long for Joshua to spot me and drive over to the house and pick me up. Together we sat on the tractor seat and continued plowing up the soil. He told me he was getting it ready for planting the late summer/early fall crops. Then he let me drive the tractor! WOW, I loved it! He taught me how to make a straight row and how to watch out for snakes. Snakes were important to help keep the rats under control. I tried not to run over any snakes. However, snakes are good at hiding and living under ground. Sometimes they would get caught-up by the tractor's tires, and then they would climb up onto the tractor and, sometimes, into the seat. That was always interesting. Joshua would just pick them up by the tail and toss them back out into the field. I never learned how to do that. Joshua taught me a lot of things, but he never taught me how to handle snakes. Some were poisonous, but most were just non-poisonous snakes, called corn snakes.

After we finished plowing the back part of the field, we went inside Joshua's house. The inside was as old as the outside. Plus, I discovered his bathroom was outside, not inside. His bathroom was an out-house, way off in the back of the yard. Joshua's room was like magic! Joshua had collected tons of books. His books covered the walls, like paint. Joshua was smart, REAL smart. His books were a collection of information on almost every topic. The books were being tossed away by the local school. Joshua took all he could get. He had history, math, science, grammar, reading, and lots of adventure books. I also discovered that Joshua also wrote his own books. He had a stack of notebooks full of stories he had written. As I scanned through his notebooks, I discovered page after page of great stories. Joshua told me he was going to be a doctor, but I knew he was going to be a writer.

As I read through his stories, one was different. One story was not fiction. It was like a journal of what he did. It caused me to stop. The title of the story was, "The Mountain People."

It was a story about the mountain people who lived deep in the woods behind Joshua's farm. Joshua told me the story was true, every word. In his story he wrote about how one day when he was plowing the field at the very back of the farm he saw a small boy. The boy was standing at the edge of the woods. He looked to be about five years old. He was dirty, very dirty. He was so dirty that, at first, Joshua thought the boy was an animal, then he realized it was a small boy. The boy looked lost, maybe homeless. The boy waved at Joshua, and Joshua waved back.

Joshua stopped the tractor, climbed down, and walked over to where the boy was standing. The boy did not run away or even move. He didn't say a word. He just held out his hand as if he needed help. Joshua took the small boy's hand and was going to take him to Sister. Then the boy froze and started pulling Joshua in the other direction, back toward the woods. Joshua had heard stories about the mountain people, and how they lived deep in the woods. The men at the country store told Joshua to **NEVER** try to find them. He was told that they were like animals. All Joshua knew about the mountain people were the stories the men at the store had told him. The mountain people were very private and could be very aggressive toward strangers. But they stayed to themselves. They didn't like or trust outsiders. They could walk through the mountains and never be seen.

Joshua assumed the little boy must have been from the mountain people's village. He must have been lost, so Joshua held the small boy's hand and walked with him back into the woods. He asked the boy what his name was, but the boy didn't reply. Either he couldn't talk or he didn't understand. Joshua continued to hold the boy's hand and, together, they walked deeper and deeper into the woods. All this time Joshua knew he shouldn't be doing what he was doing.

They walked a long way, too long! The boy and Joshua were soon deep in the woods when Joshua realized that he had gone too far. He was hopelessly lost. Suddenly the little boy let go of Joshua's hand and started running.

Then the boy stopped and pointed at an old rope bridge. It was very old and looked unsafe for anyone to use. The bridge crossed over a huge and endlessly deep ravine that separated their village from the rest of everything. The small boy stood there at the rope bridge. Suddenly two men stepped out from behind some trees. Each of the men carried a long spear and a knife. Joshua froze. He didn't know what to do or what to say. But the boy spoke to the men in their own language. The men then put down their spears and each gave Joshua a hug. Using their language, they thanked Joshua for returning the small boy.

It just so happened that this small boy was the son of the chief of the mountain tribe and had been missing for over a week. Joshua was a hero, but he was also lost, and it was getting dark. The small boy motioned for Joshua to follow him and cross the rope bridge. The boy went first and then motioned for Joshua to follow. It didn't look safe, and he had been told to NEVER go into their village. But he realized he didn't have a choice. It was too dark to find his way back home, and if he got lost deep in the woods, no one would ever find him. So, he slowly inched his way across the old rope bridge. Step-by-step Joshua watched the old rope bridge as it stretched and bent. He wondered if it would support his weight. The men waited for the little boy and Joshua to cross. Then they quickly disappeared back into the woods. Joshua was now where the men at the store told him to never go. He was deep in the woods, and in the village of the mountain people.

Once Joshua was on the other side everyone welcomed him. He was the hero who brought back one of their lost children. Joshua was now welcomed into their village as one of their children. Joshua was given food and all the children wanted him to play games with them. Joshua was now a mountain child. In the morning one of the Elders took Joshua back across the bridge and guided him back out of the woods and toward his home. As soon as Joshua saw his tractor, the Elder disappeared back into the woods. Joshua climbed onto his tractor and drove back to the barn.

Joshua wrote in his notebook that Sister saw him coming and walked out onto the porch. She was very angry and scared. She yelled, "Okay, you were gone all night. You scared me to death. Where were you?"

Joshua told her about the boy and how he met the mountain people. He told her that he was now welcomed as one of their children. Joshua wrote in his journal about how the mountain people were different from us. He wrote that they reminded him of ancient American Indian tribes he had read about. They lived together like one big family. Some wore clothes, some didn't. All the children belonged to everyone. Everything was shared, especially food. The children always ate first, in case there wasn't enough for everyone. All the women looked after the children and cooked for everyone. The younger men were hunters, and the older men were called Elders.

Joshua wrote that he was one of only two people who had been allowed to cross the rope bridge and see their world. According to the men at the store, the only person allowed to cross the rope bridge had been Doc Martin. Doc was very old and retired from his practice, but he would help the mountain people when someone was sick or hurt. When he went to help, he took pictures. The mountain people thought his camera was part of his medicine. Doc Martin's pictures and Joshua's secret notebook were the only real proof that the mountain people existed. Everything else about the mountain people was nothing more than stories told by the old men who sat and talked at the country store. Their stories, over time, became more and more exaggerated, more and more unbelievable.

Joshua wrote in his book that when he walked with the small boy back into the woods the boy was lost. The boy was not familiar with the woods, and it took all day for them to reach the village. However, when one of the Elders brought him back home, it only took about an hour.

This told Joshua that the Elders knew every tree in the woods, and the mountain people also lived very close to his house. They could watch Joshua as he worked around the farm, but Joshua would not be able to see them.

Joshua knew how hungry they were and at the end of every day he put some of his crop next to the edge of the woods. In the morning it was always gone. Joshua was afraid to tell anyone. However, one day Sister saw what he was doing, and it scared her. She had heard stories about the mountain people all her life. She was just glad that Joshua was home alive. However, she knew the mountain people would be watching Joshua. She also knew that the mountain people might come at night and take Joshua back into the woods, and this time not let him return. He had gotten too close. They now considered him one of their children. They also might think Joshua would tell people about their village and where it was. This scared Sister, but she tried hard not to show her fear.

Sister told Joshua that everything would be okay, but Joshua knew things would never be okay. Once a person was accepted into the village he became a part of the village. Joshua, I discovered, was now living in two worlds. Joshua wrote about the mountain people, but never talked about them. He wrote about how he could now feel the mountain people watching him from the woods as he plowed the fields. Joshua wrote about things he never told anyone. Joshua never told anyone about his experience deep in the woods with the mountain people, **NO ONE!** Until one day he told me everything.

Chapter #11

Joshua and I were sitting on UT's side porch, using his 22-rifle to shoot cans off the top of UT's old car. Suddenly he stopped shooting, put his rifle down, and started talking about the mountain people. I just sat and listened.

Joshua said, "Little A, do you want to go see the mountain people?" He told me that he had been back to visit the mountain people many times, but he never told Sister. Sister was deathly afraid that one day the mountain people would take Joshua from her. She told Joshua that if that happened she didn't think she could go on living, so he decided not to tell her anything. He didn't want to upset her.

I asked him if it were safe. Joshua paused for a few minutes, then told me that as long as I was with him it should be safe. However, just to make sure, on his next trip to their village he would ask the Elders for their permission. Mountain people, especially the men, the Elders, didn't like or trust outsiders. However, I was Joshua's friend and a child. But, mountain people have their own rules. Joshua just wanted to make sure it was okay for me to join him.

After Joshua and I talked about me visiting the mountain people, nothing happened. Joshua had to wait for them to contact him, and, after our talk on UT's porch, they stopped coming to Joshua's farm. It was as if he were no longer welcomed. Maybe the mountain people were closer to UT's cabin than we knew and heard us talking. All I knew was they stopped coming to Joshua's farm. It was as if Joshua were no longer to be trusted. Maybe he was no longer considered a part of their village.

Weeks passed, and I stopped thinking about the mountain people. Life on the mountain with UT returned to normal. Joshua and I were once again busy doing our everyday chores, and the mountain people were almost forgotten.

Joshua and I were now like brothers. We started hanging out together all the time. However, hanging out in the mountains was not the same as hanging out in the city. Hanging out in the mountains meant when I was at his house I helped him with his chores. And, when Joshua was at my house, he helped me with my chores.

My number one job for the summer was to split and stack firewood. Uncle Thomas needed five yards of cut, split, and stacked firewood to last him through the winter. That is a lot of firewood! It's about the length of a basketball court and stacked about six feet high.

THAT IS A LOT OF WOOD TO SPLIT AND STACK! However, to not split and stack that much wood would cause UT serious problems. If UT had a very cold and long winter, he might run out of wood. Once winter came, he had to constantly feed the wood burning stove, Annie. At his age this was serious. Uncle Thomas was now too old to cut and stack his own wood. During the winter, the roads were always covered with snow and ice. Fire wood became my number one assignment for the summer.

Chopping wood was not a game, it was serious, and it was hard. I had never split wood before. My hands soon became covered in blisters. My arms and back hurt all the time. And even with Joshua's help, I didn't know if I would be able to cut enough firewood to last UT all winter. This bothered me, but I didn't say anything to Uncle Thomas. He gave me a job to do, and I was going to do it. UT never asked if I were okay or hurt or anything. At times it was as if he didn't care or even know I was there. However, one night, while taking my bath, he noticed how skinny I had become. He asked me if I felt okay. I assured him that I was fine. I told him I was just getting down to my fighting weight. Living in the city, and eating city type fast foods, had caused me to put on too much weight. When I first met Joshua, he looked like all skin and bones, and now I was the same way. I was all skin and bones and blisters, but I had never been happier. Living with Uncle Thomas was like being an adult. He never told me to do things. Somehow, I just saw what needed to be done and did it. UT never praised me. He expected me to behave properly and didn't treat me as a child. I learned everything by watching UT and hearing what he DIDN'T say. He was a great teacher. He had high expectations of me and assumed I would say something if I were ever in trouble. Then it finally happened. One day, while walking home from Joshua's house, I got into some serious trouble. I got myself in some BIG BEAR TROUBLE.

I had never seen a bear up close before. UT told me that I almost turned white, then he laughed. He always laughed. But, to me, it was not funny. **IT WAS A BIG BEAR! IT WAS A VERY BIG GRAY BEAR!**

I was walking home from Joshua's house. I was alone on the dirt road when I saw UT at a distance coming toward me. Smokie, the forest ranger, had just told UT that a large gray bear had been spotted coming close to UT's cabin. Bears do not come close to people and cabins unless they are hungry. UT knew I was in trouble but didn't say anything. He didn't want me to panic and run. Just as soon as I saw UT, I also heard the roar of a bear. It was coming out of the woods from behind me, and it was HUGE!

UT had told me that there were bears in the mountains, but they usually avoided people. He also told me that if I ever came across a bear, DO NOT RUN. Bears can easily outrun people. And any running would cause a bear to go into its hunt and kill mode.

But, when I saw that bear come out of the woods, and how HUGE it was, I couldn't help myself. I STARTED RUNNING! And, as soon as I did that, the bear took off running after me.

The faster I ran, the faster the bear ran. I could not run any faster and the bear grew closer and closer with every step. He was right at my back. I could actually smell his fowl breath. That was when I heard UT yelling. He yelled, **"ABRAHAM, GET DOWN! GET ON THE GROUND! ABRAHAM GET DOWN! ------- NOW!"**

I looked up the road and saw UT. He was slowly pulling his pistol, the big one, the one with the long barrel, out of his holster. Using both hands he pointed it in my direction. I fell to the ground and covered my head with both arms. The bear was standing on its back legs right over me. Then I heard one shot, just one. It sounded like a canon going off. I heard the bear made a loud crying sound. Then I watched as it turned and fell on the road next to me.

UT's bullet had gone through the bear's left eyeball and out the back of its head. It killed the bear instantly.

If UT had missed, the bear would have killed me. I looked over at the bear lying in the road next to me with blood running out of its head. Then I looked down the road at UT, who was still standing with his gun pointed in my direction, ready for a second shot. UT was a long way down the road, but I saw a smile on his face that went from ear-to-ear. Then I heard him yell, "Abraham, you're one lucky boy. It's okay now. Come on, we need to get Smokie to help us move the bear out of the road."

As we walked side-by-side back to the cabin, Uncle Thomas didn't say much. He just put his arm around my trembling skinny body. As we slowly walked back to the cabin, all he said was, "It's okay, Abraham, everything is okay."

Then I heard UT quietly whisper to himself, "Thank you, Jesus. Thank you, Jesus." And Uncle Thomas was not a Jesus type person. One shot, just one shot from about fifty yards away saved my life. UT and I both knew it was impossible to do what he did with a pistol from that distance. He only had one chance to take a shot. Even with his huge long barreled pistol it wasn't just skill or luck, I think it was a miracle. But UT didn't believe in miracles. He told me that he was just good at what he did.

Smokie told me that the eye of the bear was the only place a bullet from a pistol could have stopped a bear that large. Smokie told me that UT hit a one-inch area from fifty yards away. He told me that UT was a good marksman, but to hit the eye of a moving bear at over fifty yards with a pistol was impossible. Call it whatever you want, UT did it.

It was a quiet supper that night. I didn't know what to say, and I noticed UT's hand shaking as he ate his food. After supper, he left the table without saying a word and climbed to the top of the ranger's tower. He sat by himself for a long time. I washed the dishes and waited for him to come down. After a long wait I finally went to bed. However, I didn't go to sleep until I heard the cabin door shut and UT was home.

Summer camp with UT was beginning to get interesting, but Uncle Thomas never changed. He never talked about the bear. He never lectured me about anything. It was as if we were equals. Words just weren't necessary. We both seemed to know what the other person was thinking. The next day was always a new beginning, and this time the new beginning began with a story from Joshua.

Word had spread around the mountain about how Uncle Thomas killed a giant gray bear with one shot, and it was true. UT did kill the bear with one shot. However, that wasn't all the story. The next day Joshua and I were splitting more firewood for UT when he told me something I didn't know. He said, "Little A, do you remember after UT shot the bear he called Smokie to help move it off the road?"

I told Joshua, "Yeah."

Joshua then told me that Ranger Smokie called him to bring his tractor to help drag the bear off the road and down the mountain. Joshua said when he got there, the bear was gone. Joshua heard something over in the woods, and then saw several mountain men carrying the bear away through the woods. There was enough meat there to last them a long time. Also, they would use the bear hide for shoes and clothing.

Then Joshua reached into his pocket and pulled out seven arrow heads. "Little A," he said, "I found these on the road next to where the bear was killed. I think the mountain people were leaving you a gift. I think they left these arrow heads on the road for you. It's their way to let you know they are watching you."

"UT killed the bear, but the warriors also put seven arrows in the back side of the bear just as UT took his shot. Little A, I think the mountain people are everywhere, but we just can't see them. They are probably watching you, just like they are watching me. Little A, I don't know if that is good or bad."

I asked Joshua if he thought they were watching us right now. He slowly looked around at the woods surrounding Uncle Thomas' cabin, then looked back at me, "Yes, they are watching. Don't look! But I just saw a limb fall from that small tree to your right."

"So," I said?

"So, there is no wind. And most day-time animals are easy to spot. I think someone heard us, saw me looking, and moved back deeper into the woods. Yes, I think they are watching you. I just don't know why."

Joshua and I sat there for a few minutes, neither one of us saying a word. Then I said, "Well, I guess that firewood isn't going to split itself."

We each grabbed an axe and continued splitting the wood. We had a lot of wood to split and the summer was almost over. Weeks went by and Joshua and I both had chores to do. I was busy splitting wood and Joshua was plowing his land. We didn't see much of each other over the next few weeks. I had to finish getting the fire wood split, and Joshua had a fall crop to plant. Neither one of us had time to think about the mountain people. Then, early one morning, Joshua came running up the steep hill toward UT's cabin. I heard him yelling long before I saw him. He was excited about something.

Chapter #12

Joshua ran all the way from his house. He told me he saw the little boy from the village. He was just standing there watching Joshua plow the back field. The little boy motioned for him to come with him. So, once again, Joshua went with the boy back to visit the mountain people. Joshua told me that the mountain people knew all about me and the bear. And they told Joshua it was okay for me to visit, but only me. He said they wanted to thank me for the bear. Joshua asked if I still wanted to go? Then he looked over at UT and asked him if it was O.K.

UT paused, which was not like him. He looked over at me and asked, "Do you really want to go? Do you really want to take that chance? Mountain people are strange. They live by their own rules. Plus, if you have a problem, I won't be there to help you. Abraham, these mountain people are not like you and me. They live in another world. They are not to be trusted. Are you sure about this?"

I told UT, "SURE! It would be just one more summer camp adventure."

UT understood, I think. He always seemed to understand. However, he looked concerned about something. He didn't trust the mountain people. He knew they were different. He hesitated a long time, but he finally replied, "Okay, then go, but do something for me on your journey." Then UT handed me a small bottle. He said it was skunk oil. He told me to drop a little of it along the way. He told me that BB would be able to follow the scent, just in case he needed to find me. Then he said, "Go with Joshua, but you boys be careful." Then he looked over at Joshua and said, "Joshua, when you and Abraham get back, you're invited to a party. According to my calendar, Abraham has a birthday coming up. I feel like a party, and we have a lot to celebrate! Oh, and don't forget to invite Betsy."

It was still early, and Joshua was anxious to get started. I grabbed my backpack and the skunk oil, then we took off. We started running down the same dirt road that I walked on when I met Mr. Bear. I could still see the blood stains in the dirt. Joshua didn't mention anything about the bear. He was full of words about what I was going to see, and things I needed to know. He kept telling me things to do and things not to do.

He said, "Little A, the mountain people live by themselves, separate from other people. They are very primitive, almost like animals. Some wear clothes, others don't. They do not trust outsiders. At first you will be seen as an outsider. They might try to test you. If they do, look at me for help. They will watch your every move, even your eye movement. They will not understand your words. They will touch you and smell you, just like an animal does. Don't let that freak you out."

Then Joshua started telling me things that I had read in his journal. "Little A, these people have their own rules. They are very childlike and are also very dirty. Their teeth are rotten, and many of the older people don't have any teeth. They don't take baths like we do, so get ready for the smell. If you feel scared, do not let them see that in your expression. They do not like the world outside of their mountain. They do not trust people, especially adults. They want to stay hidden and be left alone. If you have a camera, do NOT take pictures. They are very private people. They invited me to come into their village only because I am still a child, and a boy who saved one of their children."

"There is one more thing, Little A. We do not want to make the mountain people angry. They will love you and protect you as one of their own children. But, if they see any sign of anger from you, they might turn on you. Their form of punishment is swift and brutal. Remember, these are people who never leave the woods, never."

Joshua was not making my first trip to meet the mountain people sound like fun. However, I was curious about the mountain people. I was getting ready to meet people who lived by themselves deep in the mountains of Virginia, people who did not know anything about my world. I knew that the mountain people were different, but I also knew that there was a lot I had to learn about all kinds of people. I was anxious and a little scared. But Uncle Thomas was giving me a very special summer camp experience. He gave me total freedom to learn. UT never stopped me from exploring and learning. Uncle Thomas was able to read and hear my thoughts. I don't know how he did it, but, somehow, he seemed to always know where I was and what I was doing. But, was this trip into the woods too much?

There was a lot going on that I didn't understand. Summer camp with UT was a lot more than just summer camp. Uncle Thomas was, in his own unique way, teaching me things about life. He didn't teach me like they taught in school. No, he let me have the freedom to learn on my own. He was there. He was always there, but he didn't get in the way of learning. Learning had to be something I experienced on my own. It was both good and bad, but this was how life was designed. Uncle Thomas was a brave teacher, a good teacher, a teacher who was willing to let me just have the freedom to learn from life.

Chapter #13

As Joshua and I approached the village, I almost changed my mind. I was standing in the deep woods. This was a part of the Virginia mountains that no one ever visited. I was going to a place many people told to never go. However, as Joshua helped me cross over the old rope bridge we were both welcomed. The adults saw us walking toward their village and welcomed us. It was the most unreal thing I had ever experienced. I could feel the love and protection from all the adults. Children, all children, were special. Once we crossed over the rope bridge we were now their children and part of their family.

This was both interesting and scary. They ate only one meal a day, and served food that I didn't want to eat. They served any animal they could catch, ANY! That night they served cooked rats. To them rats were easy to catch and good protein. They also served worms and bugs cooked in animal fat. I looked over at Joshua for help. With his eyes, he motioned for me to eat. And with my eyes, I told him I was going to be sick. But I ate. At first, I thought I really was going to be sick, but I didn't get sick. I did what I had to do. Eating rats was normal to the mountain people, same as eating chicken. And I knew that while we were in their village I had to follow their rules. Still, Joshua kept looking at me. He didn't want me to do anything that would cause the mountain people to turn on us. The mountain people were very much like animals themselves. It was like stepping back in time a million years.

When night came we were taken into a large tent where all the children slept. The adults took turns standing watch. They were very protective of all children. The children belonged to everyone. The mountains had lots of wild animals and poisonous snakes. At night all the children were together and safe. The smell was unbearable because no one took baths. They all used the smoke from the large campfire as their bath and to keep away insects and illness. Amazingly, very few children ever got sick. It made me wonder if taking baths and being clean might be the cause of people getting sick. Were we washing off a part of our natural immune system? It was interesting, even if it did smell bad. The next morning there was dancing and laughter and happiness.

It was a special day celebrating Joshua, the boy who returned the chief's son, and Abraham, the boy who gave them the bear. There were lots of people dancing, and there was great happiness. The whole day was like a huge party. But just when things were going great, something changed. I suddenly got a taste of what Uncle Thomas was worried about.

It was in the afternoon when I saw the village chief for the first time. He came out of a large tent at the far end of the village, and he looked angry. He wanted to know who allowed me to cross the bridge. No one answered. Everyone looked scared. Standing next to him was the little boy. It was all very confusing, so Joshua and I just stood there. When the chief came out of his tent, everyone got quiet. Even the children stopped playing. The chief walked over to where Joshua and I were standing. Then he looked at me and said, "You-boy-who-live- with-crazy-man?"

I told him that I was. I nodded my head up and down. Then he yelled at me, "DID THE CRAZY MAN SEND YOU HERE?"

I shook my head, NO. Then he yelled again, "DID THE GODS OF DEATH SEND YOU HERE? Why are you here? You will bring others."

I did not understand anything, and suddenly Joshua looked scared. Joshua walked over to where I was standing. He whispered to me, "I don't like this. Something is wrong. We need to leave."

Then the chief shouted, "I AM THE GOD OF THE VILLAGE, NOT YOU!"

This was when I noticed all the village people had formed a large circle, like a wall, around the camp. I tried to talk to the people, but they didn't understand my words. I realized that Joshua and I were trapped. The little boy told Joshua that I was welcome, but maybe it was all a trap and we were caught. I looked around to see what our options were. In the distance I saw the old rope bridge. It was the only way to enter or leave the village. Joshua stepped closer to me and said, "Little A, I'm getting a bad feeling."

I looked at Joshua and said, "Go figure! I'm getting that same feeling. So, what do we do?"

Joshua looked at me and said, "Do you think we can make it to the bridge?"

I said, "Nope!"

The rope bridge was on the other side of the village from where we were standing. Even if we made it, we would face two Elders who guarded the bridge. No one crossed the bridge without their approval. It was a very interesting trap, and we had been caught. At first Joshua and I were treated like special guest. However, right after the chief came out of his tent, things began to go downhill. Then, just when we thought things couldn't get any worse, they got worse!

Suddenly the chief looked up at the sky and said something to the Elders. Then all the Elders got together and started arguing and shouting. Something was wrong, and the Elders kept pointing at me and yelling. That was when I noticed what was wrong. It was starting to get dark, and it was only afternoon. The Elders were scared. The Elders started yelling at Joshua and me. They thought I was causing the sun to go out.

Joshua suddenly realized what we were experiencing. Joshua exclaimed with fear in his voice, "OH NO! It's an eclipse, and there's no way I can explain this to the chief and Elders. We're in deep trouble and it's only going to get deeper as things get darker."

Joshua looked over at me and said, "Little A, I think we are dead meat."

The chief was angry, very angry. He told the Elders that I had caused the Sun to go out. We were now in DOUBLE BIG trouble, and Joshua and I had to think quickly.

Joshua and I looked around. The village men pulled out their knives and formed a small circle around where we were standing. As the Sun slowly went behind the moon, the village people froze with fear. That was when I yelled at Joshua, "WE HAVE TO RUUUUUUUN, BROTHER! WE HAVE TO RUN FOR THE BRIDGE, NOW!"

Then Joshua yelled, "O.K., LETS GO FOR IT!" Once we started running, it was just like the bear story. They were right behind us. But then it suddenly went totally dark. The village people didn't know what to do, and once again they froze. I yelled over at Joshua, "**KEEP RUNNING!!!!!!**" And we both ran for our lives.

Then I heard Joshua yell, "**WE'LL NEVER MAKE IT. IT'S TOO FAR.**"

When the sky went dark, the village people were terrified. The young men in the village, the hunters, all started running after us. The hunters are very fast runners, and I knew we were not going to make it to the bridge, so I stopped. I told Joshua to stay where he was, and I slowly walked back into the camp. The mountain people thought I had some kind of magic power and made the Sun go out. I had to make them think I could bring it back.

All I had to do was kill time until the eclipse was over. So, I started dancing around the large campfire, like I had seen Indians do in the movies. Everyone stopped and watched. I knew if I could keep them calm for just a few minutes the Sun would start to come out again. So, I danced and danced and danced. I tried to look like Michael Jackson. I was moon walking and doing robot moves. I did everything I could think of to keep them calm (or entertained). I made loud yelling sounds, pointed to the sun, and started tossing my clothes into the fire, like a sacrifice to the sun god. I was doing everything I could do to make then think I was controlling the Sun. It sounds corny, but it seemed to be working. While dancing around the fire and tossing my clothes into the fire as a sacrifice, the Elders started sacrificing their clothes. I tossed my shirt into the fire and watched it go up in flames, then my pants, then my socks and shoes. However, I was running out of clothes and it was still dark. My boxers were the last thing I tossed into the fire. I was standing there, with all the Elders, yelling at the Sun. Suddenly the Sun started coming out from behind the moon. I started clapping my hands and motioned for everyone to clap their hands. Everyone responded. They all stood frozen, watching the Sun reappear while clapping their hands. Now was the time for Joshua and me to make our move. Once again, we both started running toward the rope bridge.

But the Elders, who guarded the bridge, were standing in our way. They pulled out their knives to stop us. There was no way we were going to get past them. That was when I heard the cannon going off. I looked across the ravine and there stood UT with his big pistol, the one with the long barrel, and Ranger Smokie. UT shot his pistol up in the air, and the Elders guarding the bridge ran away.

Joshua and I started running across the bridge. We were about half way across when the Elders started shouting at us and then started cutting the rope that held the bridge. Suddenly, I could feel the bridge starting to move.

Joshua yelled for me to run faster, but we weren't fast enough. I could hear the knives chopping at the rope bridge. Then I felt the bridge drop out from under my feet. For a few minutes I was floating in air, then I was falling to my death. As I fell, I caught hold of a part of the old rope bridge, and Joshua caught hold of my left leg. We were hanging about six feet down. I could see the old rope bridge beginning to come apart from the weight of both of us. In my last minutes of life, all I could think about was how UT was going to explain this to my mom. Then I heard Joshua. He YELLED, "**Little A, I wonder how far down we're going to fall?**"

Just then I felt the wind of an arrow as it passed by my body and stick in the ground next to where I was hanging. Then there was another arrow, and another. Joshua and I were hanging from a rope bridge while the mountain people started shooting arrows at us.

I YELLED at Joshua, **"I don't think we are going to have to worry about falling."**

Then, once again, I heard the cannon, and the arrows stopped. I felt a large rope hit my back. I looked up and saw UT and Smokie leaning over the edge looking down at us. UT yelled, "Hold on to the rope, we have a birthday party to go to."

He just looked down at us as if hanging from an old rope bridge were normal. He wasn't angry or excited or anything. All he said was, "Little A, where are your clothes?"

I yelled back, **"I HAD TO SACRIFICE MY CLOTHES TO THE SUN GOD IN ORDER TO SAVE OUR LIVES!"**

UT replied, **"Abraham, I don't know who is crazier, you or me."**

Then UT and Smokie pulled us up the side of the mountain, and we all started our long walk back to UT's cabin, as BB and Smokie led the way. They were following the skunk oil. That was how UT knew where to find us.

I asked UT why he came looking for me. He told me that Smokie talked him into it. He didn't want to, but Smokie knew how dangerous the mountain people could be. Smokie thought it would be a good idea to just make sure we were okay, and I am sure glad he did!

Yes, summer camp with UT was different. It was totally awesome! That night we had a birthday party, a BIG birthday party! And Betsy surprised me with a pink birthday cake. After eating some of my birthday cake, I paused. UT told me that I just sat there looking around the room. I saw UT, Smokie, Joshua, Betsy, BB, and ...., and then I fell asleep.

Yes, I fell asleep while sitting up at the table eating my pink birthday cake. My face just fell into the cake. UT picked me up, wiped off my face, and laid me in bed. I was a very tired thirteen- year-old birthday boy. UT told me that everyone sang happy birthday to me while I slept, and then went home. The birthday party was over.

Chapter #14

The next day I realized I hadn't looked at my computer all summer, not once. Also, I hadn't written any book reports for Mom. However, thanks to Uncle Thomas, I had read a lot of books.

I didn't miss the computer! I was too busy working and having fun. I was too busy learning about life. And at times, I was too busy just surviving. There wasn't any time for a computer. In fact, I learned how unimportant computers were when it came to chopping wood, plowing fields, making bread, shooting a rifle, and taking baths in a tin tub. If UT had taken my computer away from me when I first arrived, I would have been furious. But, as always, he said nothing and just let me discover a world without computers on my own.

Many times, when I think back on my summer camp experience with UT, I think what a great summer assignment that would be for teachers to give their students. For the entire summer ask your students to not look at a computer or TV. This is what I did, and I loved the experience. I read books, chop/split fire wood, out run a bear, made the Sun disappear, and took a bath in a tin tub (with everyone watching). And then I wrote a book about my experience.

This is what I did. I wrote a book about everything. However, I didn't start writing my book until I got home. While at Uncle Thomas' cabin there was too much work that needed to be done. My number one assignment was to split enough firewood for UT.

This assignment started out as fun, as long as Joshua helped me. We talked, laughed, sang stupid songs, and split wood. However, the summer was moving by in a hurry and I was a long way from getting enough firewood to last Uncle Thomas through the winter. The fun part was over, and the work days now started early and lasted until it was dark. Every muscle in my body hurt. All I could see was a large empty space that had to be full of fire wood before I went home.

Uncle Thomas never said a word. I created my own work schedule. I had to have enough wood to last Uncle Thomas through the winter. I could not go home knowing that I had not done what I was asked to do. It was the first feeling I ever had of being an adult. There were no excuses. There were no thoughts of not getting the job done. I had to do it and I was determined to do it.

UT never said a word. Some days he would sit on his side porch and watch me. Some nights I was too tired to eat. He never said a word. He was teaching me about life. What he was teaching me could not be learned in a classroom or from a book. It could only come from facing the impossible, and then doing it. I learned something on the mountain top that changed my life. I learned that everything is possible if you want it hard enough.

Then, early one morning, I heard someone splitting firewood. It wasn't me, I was still in bed. It wasn't UT, he was fixing breakfast. I crawled out of bed and opened the door. When I stepped outside there were lots of men, Elders, chopping wood. And there, sitting on a tree stump was the little boy. UT said that they were there before the sun came up. He told me that they probably would not stop until the job was done. I asked if I could help. He said, "Sure. I think they would like that."

I looked over at the little boy. He waved. I waved back, grabbed my axe, and joined the men. Soon more men walked out of the woods and started helping. I looked over at the little boy, he was laughing. By the end of the day there was more than enough firewood for UT.

Just as quickly as the men had arrived, they left. The men walked back into the woods. I never saw them again. The little boy walked over to UT and, to my surprise, spoke perfect English. He told UT that their Sun burned out and I brought it back. He told UT if he needed more wood, just tell Joshua.

I didn't understand. Not long ago they tried to kill me and now they thanked me. UT told me that they were mountain people, they were good people. They just didn't understand a lot of things. When the Sun went dark they thought it was my fault. And, when it came back, they thought it was something I did.

Uncle Thomas told me that he was proud of how hard I had worked all summer. He said, "Abraham, it's now time for us to have some fun."

I told Uncle Thomas that I was already having fun. I didn't understand why or how splitting fire wood could be fun, but it was. I was down to my fighting weight and getting some muscles. I welcomed help from the mountain people. As hard as I worked, I could not have split enough wood on my own. UT knew this and didn't say anything. He just watched. I think he wanted to see how I would react when I didn't reach my goal. Would I get angry? Would I cry? Would I blame it on someone else?

Once again Uncle Thomas taught me another lesson. We all need a little help at times, and we all need friends who will help us. I learned so much from UT, but the summer was almost over. One morning when I walked out onto the side deck I could feel the chill in the air. Everything just smelled different. That was the day I realized that summer camp was over.

Chapter #15

Uncle Thomas let me drink coffee, and it tasted great early in the morning. UT and I would sit on the deck, drink our coffee, and talk about everything. However, on that morning, I sat by myself sipped at my coffee as tears slowly started rolled down my face. I didn't want to go home, but I knew I had to. It was time for UT to be by himself again. I think he was ready. He didn't tell me this, I could just sense it. Uncle Thomas was old. He was used to living by himself. He and I, over the summer, had become more like brothers than nephew and uncle. Over the summer we bonded in a way that could only have happened on the top of a mountain somewhere in Virginia.

I think I learned that less was more. I learned that the less I had the happier I was. I also learned that being needed was important. Splitting firewood for UT was an impossible challenge for a small city boy. However, when I finished, I felt like I had become a man. I did something that was important, and I did it for someone who needed my help.

I think I learned that school was everywhere. All I had to do was LOOK. I sat on the porch and thought about the first book I learned to read. It was a book called,

LOOK and SEE. That first book taught me how to read simple sight words. This summer I turned thirteen, and I am still learning about sight words. I am still learning how to LOOK and how to SEE. That was when I saw a car coming up UT's driveway.

It was a police car pulling up the steep hill toward UT's cabin. I didn't know what to expect. When the officer got out of his car, he just stood there and looked at everything. When I walked out the front door of the cabin I immediately recognized him. It was the same policeman who stopped us as we were leaving Memphis. He had a big smile. He looked over at me and said, "Boy, you've changed a lot this summer. You look different."

I walked over to where he was standing and asked, "Am I in trouble?"

"No Abraham, you are not in trouble, but your uncle won't look at his computer, and he doesn't have a phone. Your mom sent another message to the police department to find you and bring you home before school started. She must think all we do is find children. However, my boss gave me permission to drive all the way to Virginia to find you."

I looked up at him and said, "You drove all the way from Memphis just to find me?"

"Yep, all the way. You have become a hero, and so has your mom."

UT invited the officer to come inside where we all sat and talked. It wasn't long before Joshua walked in the front door. Joshua saw the police car as it passed by his house and turned up the road that lead to UT's cabin. He wanted to make sure everything was okay.

Joshua pointed at me, "Little A, you're in big trouble, aren't you?"

The police officer looked over at Joshua and asked, "Who are you?"

Joshua replied, "I am Little A's mountain brother." Just then Betsy came running through the doorway. The officer looked at her and asked, "And, young lady, who are you?" All she said was, "Betsy."

The officer said, "Well, I am sorry, mountain brother, but his mom has asked me to bring your brother home. School begins in just two weeks. Do you want to go?"

Joshua paused, then he said, "Yes. I want to go, but I can't. I have to stay and look after Sister and help feed the mountain people." Then Joshua looked over at me.

There was a lot he wanted to say, but all he said was, "Little A, there is a lot you don't know about me. I never lied to you, but I also never told you the whole truth, the truth about me and the mountain people. After my parents died, and Sister adopted me, I stayed on the farm and started noticing that our crops were disappearing at night. Then one day I saw the little boy. He was almost starved to death. I gave him some food, and from that day on I have worked the farm to help feed the mountain people. If it weren't for Sister and me they would probably starve to death. I don't think I will ever leave the farm or the mountains. Too many people depend on me, especially Sister. She is getting old. She doesn't talk much anymore. Sometimes she forgets my name. Betsy does all the house work and cooking. She and I run the store. I take care of the farm and the crops. Sister now spends her days in her bedroom. She sits in a chair and stares out the window. Betsy and I bathe her and feed her and love her."

Suddenly the room grew silent. I didn't know what to say. There was a long pause. I could see tears starting to run down Joshua's face. I remained speechless. Then Joshua asked in almost a whisper, "Will you come back next summer?" Then Betsy said, **"please."**

"Sure," I said, "Sure, I wouldn't miss it for the world. What color paint should I bring?" We all tried to laugh but couldn't.

Joshua didn't say another word. He couldn't say another word. His words were frozen in thought. He waved a stupid little wave, and I gave him the finger. We both started laughing. We had to laugh. Things were getting too serious for two young boys. Then Joshua and Betsy turned and walked out the door.

In a few minutes Joshua ran back inside. He YELLED, **"Have you seen what's on the top of UT's car?"** We all hurried outside. There, covering the top of UT's old car, was a perfect gray bear skin, a gift from the mountain people to me. I went over and crawled up on top of UT's car. I lay down on top of the bear skin. I knew they were watching. I set up and waved at the woods. I knew they were there somewhere, watching. That was when I saw him, the little boy. He waved good-by, turned, and ran back into the woods.

UT told me to gather up all my stuff and get in the officer's car. Then he thanked me for all his firewood. He hugged me, turned, and slowly started climbing the steps to the top of the fire tower.

But I noticed something different about Uncle Thomas. For the first time he looked old. He was moving slower than usual. Then I noticed what was different. He wasn't wearing his pistol. He always wore his huge pistol, the one with the long barrel. He only took it off to take a bath.

As the officer and I drove down the steep mountain road, I could see UT standing on the top of the tower, next to Smokie. He waved good-bye.

I waved good-bye. Neither one of us could say good-bye. Summer camp was over. In a few weeks I would be starting the eighth grade.

On the first day of school, the teachers always asked every student to write a report on their summer vacation. Then we had to stand up and read our paper to the class. I could hardly wait.

The End

Postscript

I wrote my report for the teacher, and then read it to the class. After turning in my two pages, I asked the teacher if I could write a few more pages about my summer vacation. He said, "Sure, how many more pages do you want to write?" I told him I didn't know, maybe ninety or a hundred or a thousand. I told him it was a summer I had to write about.

It was the summer that I came of age.

He just sat there at his desk and began to smile, and, for a long time, didn't say a word. Then he stood up and said, "Abraham, let me show you something." He walked over to his filing cabinet and pulled out a folder. The folder was old, yellowish, and torn. It had about ninety to a hundred hand written pages inside. He said, "I wrote this when I was your age. This is my story, my coming of age. It is the most important thing I own, so I understand. Abraham, write your story. And, Abraham, don't write it for a grade, write it for yourself."

And that is what I did. This is my coming of age story.

About the Author, "Mr. Chip"

Shirley Nelson Kersey, Ph.D.

Readers of the books of fiction featuring Little A, a boy living in the projects of Memphis, are instantly aware that the writer is eminently qualified to focus on this young hero.Only a person who has taught in the inner city schools is able to create a fictional, yet realistic account of the life of a youngster struggling to find himself in this environment.

John Chipley, whom the boys fondly have dubbed Mr. Chip, taught in Memphis inner-city schools for over fifteen years. In retirement he

offers weekly volunteer sessions that focus on encouraging boys to read. This is a lofty goal, for the boys live in homes and neighborhood

environments not structured to develop reading skills or dreams of career advancement. Mr. Chip's goal surpasses development of reading

ability to encourage the boys to enjoy this privilege.

Chipley is formally prepared to teach, for he holds both Bachelor and Master of Education degrees. However, the most memorable aspect of his classroom presence is his heart. He cares deeply about each one of his students and is there for them both now and in the future. Through the persona of Little A, Chipley gives the boys a fictional character with whom they can identify. Little A's life style echoes theirs. While reading this series of books, the boys witness someone they can relate to. Little A is a wonderful fictional character full of wisdom, character, adventure, and confidence.

List of Little A Books

WWW.johnchipley.com

- **WARNING, Vegetables can kill you**
  - Funny, funny, funny to the very last word

- **The No Good, Very Bad, Terrible, Rotten Teacher**
  - A murder mystery about hamburgers?

- **A Necessary Sin**
  - Sometimes we all sin, even at the age of twelve.

- **The Magic Shoes**
  - About basketball and Mr. Boom-Boom

- **The Dreamer**
  - "Mr. Snake." Is he a good bad guy, or a bad good guy?

- **And Ku-jaa**
  - She was beautiful, but lived in the future

Printed in the United States
By Bookmasters